```
J            $9.45
636.1        Henderson, Kathy
He               I can be a horse
             trainer
```

DATE DUE

AG 31'90	AP 20'92	MAY 02'95	SEP 08 '97
SE 19'90	AG 3'92	JUN 29 '95	SEP 20 '97
FE 21'91	OC 1'92	AUG 21 '95	
MR 21'91	OC 14'92	SEP 18 '95	JUN 30 '98
AP 22'91	MY 28'93	JAN 02 '96	JAN 28 '98
MY 22'91	SE 15'93	JUL 11 '96	JUN 20 '98
JY 15'91	APR 27 '94	AUG 06 '96	SEP 29 '98
JY 27'91	JUL 13 '94	NOV 28 '96	OCT 19 '98
SE 25'91	SEP 05 '94	JUL 09 '97	NOV 27 '98
NO 7'91	DEC 01 '94	JUL 21 '97	
NO 29'91	DEC 15 '94	JUL 30 '97	
JA 13'92	JAN 26 '95	NOV 05 '97	JY 09 '99

I CAN BE A
HORSE TRAINER

By Kathy Henderson

Prepared under the direction of Robert Hillerich, Ph.D.

CHILDRENS PRESS®
CHICAGO

Library of Congress Cataloging-in-Publication Data

Henderson, Kathy.
  I can be a horse trainer / by Kathy Henderson.
    p.   cm.
  Summary: Discusses what a horse trainer does and
how horses are trained.
  ISBN 0-516-01960-0
  1. Horses—Training—Juvenile literature. 2. Horse
trainers—Juvenile literature. [1. Horses—Training.
2. Horse trainers. 3. Occupations.] I. Title.
SF287.H46   1990
636.1'088—dc20   89-29203
                                                CIP
                                                 AC

For my daughter Amy

PICTURE DICTIONARY

gentling

cavalletti

lunge line

── GROUND TRAINING ──

lipizzaner

trotter

GAITS

walk

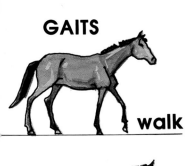

trot

gallop

haw   gee

racehorse

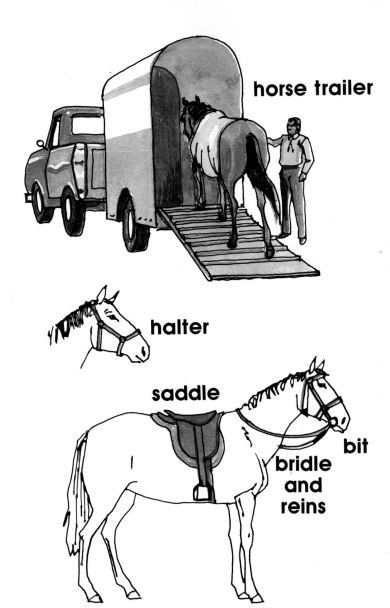

horse trailer

halter

saddle

bit

bridle
and
reins

PLEASURE HORSES

Quarter   Morgan   Arabian
horse

Students learn to ride. For safety, they wear helmets.

Have you ever ridden a horse by yourself?

Up you climb into the saddle. You hold the reins tight and bump the horse with your legs. Then you say, "Giddy up."

If your horse has been trained well, it will walk

off easily. If you know the
correct signals, you can
make your horse trot, gallop,
turn, jump, or stop by just
flicking the reins or
tapping its sides with your
foot or whispering a
command. Amazing, isn't it?

Who taught your horse
to behave so well? Would
you like to train horses
when you grow up?

walk

trot

gallop

Rider (above) teaches his horse to turn. Horses and dogs (right) can be trained to hunt animals. The famous Lipizzan horses (below right) are trained to leap into the air. Horses used to play polo (below) are taught to turn quickly.

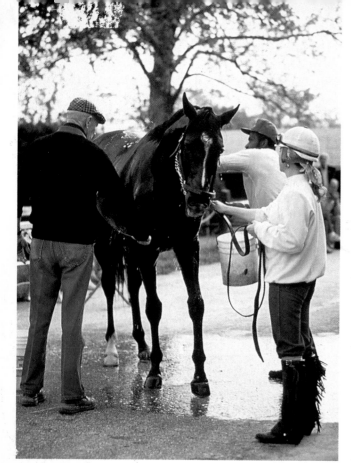

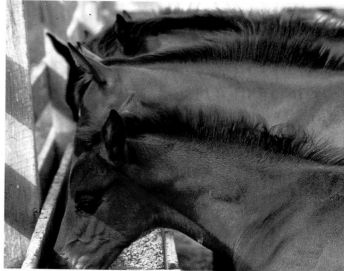

Sunday Silence (left) won the
Kentucky Derby in 1989. Racehorses
are fed special foods to keep them
strong.

Trainers must know
many things about horses.
They must know how to
feed and care for a
horse to keep it healthy.
They must know how to

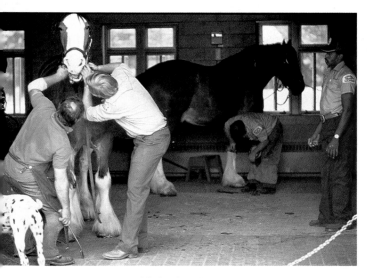

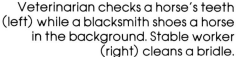
Veterinarian checks a horse's teeth (left) while a blacksmith shoes a horse in the background. Stable worker (right) cleans a bridle.

choose exactly the right equipment for every horse they train. They must know how to judge a horse so that they know what— and how—to teach it.

Ranch horses must be taught how to work with cattle.

ranch horse

Some horses make good ranch horses. Ranch horses must be able to start, stop, and turn very quickly to cut, or sort out, cattle from a herd. They must be strong. Ranch horses must carry a rider for long hours.

Some horses make good racehorses. All racehorses are slender and swift. They must have strong legs and good lungs.

racehorse

The Kentucky Derby (below left) is held at Churchill Downs in Louisville, Kentucky.

Trotter pulls a sulky.

trotter

Trotters are racehorses that pull little carts called sulkies around a track. In a steeplechase, horses race across flat ground and jump fences.

In a steeplechase,
horses race around
a course and jump
fences. Some fences
are made of wood.

Quarter horse

Arabian and Lipizzan horses

PLEASURE HORSES

Quarter   Morgan   Arabian
horse

Some horses are called pleasure horses. They can be trained to do many things. Pleasure horses are friendly and even-tempered animals. Quarter horses, Arabians, and Morgans

14

Morgan horses

make good pleasure
horses. They can be
trained to carry a saddle
and rider. They can pull
buggies and carriages.
And with a rider, they
can race against other
horses.

Horse trainers start
training a new horse
shortly after it is born.
They talk to the horse so
that it gets used to their
voice. They rub their
hands all over its body
and stroke the horse with
soft-bristled brushes.

This is called gentling. It teaches a young or untrained horse to trust the trainer and to be comfortable around people.

The trainer teaches the horse to lead. The horse

must learn to wear a
halter and how to walk
beside the trainer without
tugging or pulling. It must
learn to stop when the
trainer stops. It must also
learn to stand still without
fussing when it is tied to
a post. It must let the
trainer pick up its feet so
that dirt can be scraped
out of its hooves.

Little by little, the
trainer helps the horse

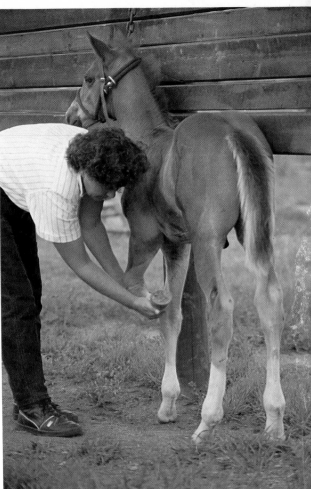

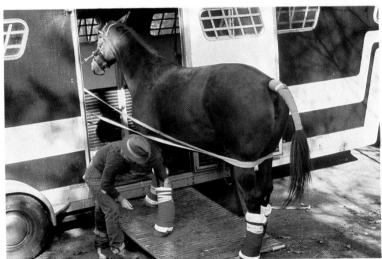

Horses learn to stand still and let people touch them.

get used to new things, such as wearing a bridle and saddle, or backing out of a trailer, or having its mane clipped.

horse trailer

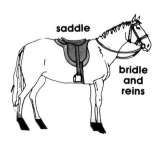

saddle

bridle and reins

A horse walks at the end of a lunge line (above). A well-trained horse (right) learns to follow many different commands.

lunge line

Often a trainer uses a "lunge line" or "bits up" the horse with a bridle that has extra long reins and trains the horse from

the ground. This is called
ground training.

The horse learns to
obey voice commands
such as "walk," "whoa,"
or "stand." The horse
also learns to turn right
when the trainer calls
"gee" and pulls gently on
one rein. The horse learns
to turn left when the
trainer calls "haw" and
pulls on the other rein.

haw   gee

Ground training is very
important. It is good
practice for the horse
and the trainer.

Soon the trainer tries
riding the horse. The
trainer uses the same

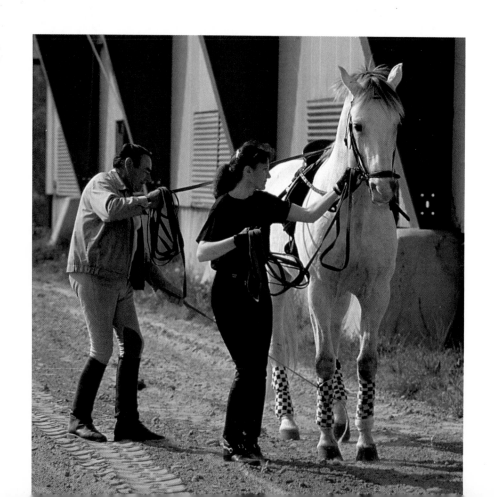

Trainers work hard to teach their horses to obey commands.

voice commands that he
or she used in ground
training. A gentle tug on
the reins will tell the
horse when to turn or
when to stop.

A horse is called "green broke" once it has learned to obey simple commands. Now it is time to "finish" the horse by teaching it the special skills it will need to do its job.

For instance, a show horse must learn to jump.

To teach a show horse to jump, the trainer first trots it over poles laid on the ground. These poles are called cavalletti. When the horse learns to step over the poles without hitting them, they are raised higher off the ground.

cavalletti

In addition to obeying voice commands and hand movements, many horses are taught to respond to their rider's leg and body movements. The horse learns what a tap from the rider's heel

A trainer shows a student how to give a horse commands with her heel.

or a shift of the rider's
position in the saddle
means. When this is done
correctly, you do not see
the rider give the horse
commands, but the horse
suddenly changes gaits,
turns, stops, backs up, or
even steps sideways.

This advanced training is called dressage. It takes both horse and trainer many years to perfect. The famous Lipizzaner horses and their trainers are masters in performing dressage movements.

Lipizzaner

Only the adult Lipizzaners are white.

There are many things
a trainer can teach a
horse to do. Each one
takes time and patience.
A trainer must love horses
enough to work with them
every day.

Do you think you could
be a horse trainer?

WORDS YOU SHOULD KNOW

bit (BIHT) — a piece of metal that goes in a
  horse's mouth

bridle (BRY • dil) — a set of leather straps that
        goes around a horse's head and has a
        metal part called a bit that goes in the
        horse's mouth.

cavalletti (kav • uh • LET • ee) — a series of
          wooden poles that are adjustable in
          height, used for training horses

dressage (dreh • SAHJ) — the training of horses
          to perform movements at small foot
          and body signals from the rider

gait (GAYTE) — a way of running or walking

gallop (GAL • up) — to go very fast with all four
        feet off the ground at the same time

halter (HAWL • ter) — a strap or rope used to tie
        or to lead an animal; a bridle without a bit

Lipizzaner (LIH • pih • zan • er) — a breed of white
          horses that first came from Spain and
          Italy. They can be trained to perform
          graceful jumping and dancing
          movements.

quarter horse (KWOR • ter   HORSE) —a type of saddle horse that has great endurance and that can start, stop, and turn quickly

reins (RAYNZ) —leather straps that are attached to a horse's bridle and held by the rider to control the animal

saddle (SAD • il) —a leather seat that is strapped on the back of a horse for the rider to sit in

steeplechase (STEE • pil • CHAISS) —a race in which the horses jump over fences

sulkies (SUHL • keez) —small, two-wheeled buggies pulled by horses in harness races

trot (TRAHT) —a two-beat gait where a horse's front leg and the opposite back leg move at the same time

trotter (TRAH • ter) —a type of horse used in harness racing

INDEX

PHOTO CREDITS

ABOUT THE AUTHOR

Kathy Henderson works closely with children, teachers, and librarians through young author conferences and workshops, and is a frequent guest speaker in schools. An experienced freelance writer with hundreds of newspaper and magazine articles to her credit, she is also the author of the *Market Guide for Young Writers* and an active member of the Society of Children's Book Writers. Mrs. Henderson lives on a 400-acre dairy farm in Michigan with her husband Keith, and two teenage children.